basic

re the date

For Guitar

Other titles by David Mead available from Sanctuary Publishing:

Basic Chords For Guitar
Basic Guitar Workout
100 Tips For Acoustic Guitar You Should Have Been Told
100 Tips For Blues Guitar You Should Have Been Told
100 Guitar Tips You Should Have Been Told
Rhythm – A Step By Step Guide To Understanding Rhythm For Guitar
10 Minute Guitar Workout
Chords & Scales For Guitarists

With Martin Taylor
Kiss And Tell – Autobiography Of A Travelling Musician

Printed and bound in Great Britain by Antony Rowe Limited, Chippenham, Wiltshire

Published in the UK by SMT, an imprint of Sanctuary Publishing Limited, Sanctuary House, 45-53 Sinclair Road, London W14 0NS, United Kingdom

www.sanctuarypublishing.com

Copyright: David Mead, 2003

Music typesetting: Cambridge Notation

ISBN: 1-86074-364-1

basic Scales
For Guitar

David Mead

smt

CONTENTS

INTRODUCTION

During the 1980s, guitarists became unnaturally attracted to the idea of learning as many scales as possible, which introduced a whole generation to the notion that there was little that was as important as being a walking scale lexicon. And, naturally, the faster you could play them, the better musician you undoubtedly were.

Now I think we've woken up to the fact that scales are nothing to do with music in a creative sense, in the same way that dictionaries don't win the Nobel Prize for literature, despite containing every word ever written. Everything you need is there, but it's up to you to put it into a creative order. You see my point? Actual knowledge of scales – that is, being aware of their different hues and timbres – is a good idea in the same way that an extended vocabulary is a great creative tool for a writer. But scales are far from being the whole story.

In this book, I've set out to put the record straight, as far as scales are concerned. Here, you'll learn simply what scales are, how they're used, the basic 'flavours' that are available and, most importantly, a few tips on how to continue building a scale vocabulary that will help you in your own creative endeavours.

David Mead

SECTION 1

1 HOW TO READ TABLATURE

The scale diagrams shown throughout this book are presented in two different ways: in tablature and as fretboard diagrams. The tablature gives you immediate access to the positions of the notes of each scale on the fretboard, whereas the diagrams will help you to visualise the complete scale shape as it lies on the guitar fretboard.

If you're at all unsure about how either tab or fretboard diagrams work, take a few moments to look through this chapter and hopefully things will soon become a lot clearer.

Left-Hand Fingering
The left-hand fingering is represented using the numbers 1, 2, 3 and 4, where the index finger is 1, the middle finger is 2, the ring finger is 3 and the little finger is 4.

Fretboard Diagrams

These diagrams borrow from the standard method of showing guitar chords for the guitar. You've perhaps seen chord boxes before, where a system of grid boxes pictorially represent the instrument's six strings, with the bass string (ie the thickest string) shown at the left-hand side, as below:

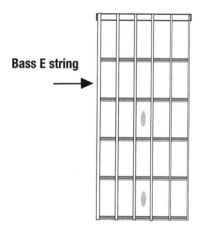

Bass E string

The finger positions are shown by black circular blobs, like this:

C major

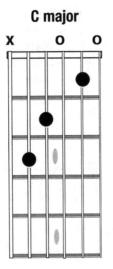

A suggested left-hand fingering is shown via numerals underneath the grid, aligned to their respective blobs, as in the diagram at the top of the next page.

In the above example, the chord concerned is C major and calls for the left-hand third finger to be placed on the A string at the third fret, the second finger to be placed on the D string at the second fret and the first finger to be placed on the B string at the first fret.

C major

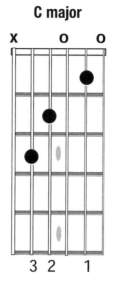

An 'o' written above an open string means that it is part of the chord and should therefore be played along with the rest of the strings. An 'x' means that you shouldn't sound the string. In general, you'll only find an 'x' on the lower strings and very rarely in the middle of a chord.

This system is adapted for scale diagrams in the following way:

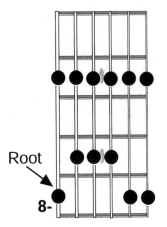

In the diagram above, the scale is represented by the same system of blobs, with the root (or starting note) indicated by an arrow.

In general, the left-hand fingering for scales calls for you to use one finger for each fret, like this:

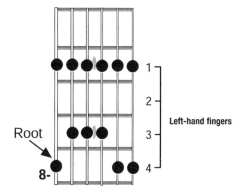

Root

1

2

Left-hand fingers

3

8-

4

If a finger has to stray out of position, it will be shown like this:

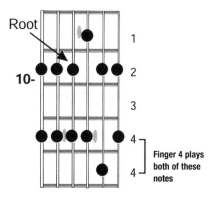

Root

1

10-

2

3

4

Finger 4 plays both of these notes

4

basic Scales For Guitar

In this instance, finger 4 has to reach for a note on the guitar's second string. These stretches are comparatively rare, but it doesn't hurt the hand to learn to accommodate an area covering five frets in some way, as long as you try not to overdo it in the early stages.

At the first sign of physical discomfort in the hand, stop and rest for a while. It's not unnatural to assume that the hand has to go through a certain amount of muscular development, in the same way that you'd expect a few aches and pains if you started some form of new exercise routine at a gym. Your muscles will need to wake up a little, particularly those in the left hand, which I'm guessing is probably not the hand you use for most of the things you do. (If you're left handed and have made the decision to play the guitar in what has become known as 'the conventional manner', I apologise!)

Watch out for the highlighted starting points, or root notes – they're not necessarily going to lie on the sixth string, and you'll very probably find yourself starting a scale in what appears to be the middle of a diagram.

You should always play the scales as they are shown

in the tab; it's important for your developing musical ear to hear the scales played from root to root. In these instances, the tab will represent your cross-check. In any case, the fretboard diagrams are valuable as a general overview of a particular scale's position on the neck.

Tablature

Melodies and scales are generally notated for the guitar using tablature. This is a system of dedicated notation that has been around for guitar players since the 16th century and is far from being the modern-day cop-out that some mistake it for.

While in most cases learning to read standard notation, or 'proper music', is unnecessary, it's a very good idea to become familiar with tablature, as this will unlock a lot of transcriptions widely available on the market today. What's more, it's extremely easy to learn, whereas learning to read music can take considerably longer.

Tablature is written on six lines, each of which represents a string of the guitar, with the bass E string shown on the bottom, as shown over the page:

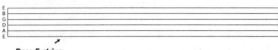

Bass E string

Fret locations are shown by a series of numbers written on the lines. In the following example, you're required to play the fifth fret on the G string, followed by the sixth fret on the B:

If two or more notes are meant to be played together, they are 'stacked' on top of each other, like this:

So a whole chord would look like this:

Occasionally, you'll see other symbols creep into tablature to inform you that a certain technique has to be employed while you play a certain note. These symbols fall outside the scope of this book, but any that might sneak in along the way will be explained in the accompanying text.

2 THE RIGHT WAY TO LEARN SCALES

There is a theory that scales were invented by some evil music teacher way back in the Middle Ages with the sole purpose of taking most of the fun out of learning music. Certainly, when I was introduced to the idea that a great deal of my leisure time had to be redirected towards learning a lot of meaningless finger exercises (as I then perceived them), I wasn't too impressed; I just wanted to play, and learning something called the C♯ harmonic minor scale seemed too high a price to pay by far. But of course I was ten at the time and learning piano, and let's face it, most ten-year-olds are blind to abstract concepts like playing scales. What's more, I hated playing piano and desperately wanted to switch to guitar, and so I taught myself to play Beethoven's 'Moonlight' sonata and The Beatles' 'Lady Madonna' instead of the stuff my piano teacher actually wanted me to play. I was never a great fan of 'D'Ye Ken John Peel', even at that tender age, so I rebelled and pretty soon the piano lessons stopped and I got a guitar for Christmas.

Of course, if my piano teacher had told me what scales were all about and why it was good for me to learn them, things might have been different.

As my interest in the guitar became more and more serious, I found myself wanting to learn every scale I could lay my hands on, because I recognised the value in introducing my ears to the basic lexicon of music and of introducing my hands to the concept of playing melody.

Since that time, I have introduced my pupils at the earliest possible opportunity to the idea that scales are good for them. What's more, I've been careful not to make learning them an arduous chore, and so I've struck deals with my students whereby I would only spend about ten minutes of each hour-long lesson dealing with scales. In return, the other 50 minutes were theirs to direct as they chose. It worked. I don't think too many of them ever really got to love playing through their scales, but they all saw that ten minutes of serious scale study each lesson was a bearable amount of time before we could get down to the more serious question of actually learning to play a song or a solo.

I'm suggesting the same sort of bargain here – learning

scales is important, but don't overdo it to the point where practising them becomes hard work. A few minutes each day is all that's needed – to begin with, at least – and this have you exercising your fingers in an extremely useful way and one that will form a very solid foundation upon which you can build the rest of your playing.

So Where Do We Start?

As far as I'm concerned, I think the most logical path to take, where scales are concerned, is to deal with the most common ones first and worry about all the fancy-sounding ones much later on. You might be wondering exactly how many scales there are in music's rather broad span. In actual fact, the answer is very far from simple.

In music, there are five-note, six-note, seven-note and eight-note scales, but they are all drawn from just one basic scale: the chromatic scale. This scale contains every note used in western music (with a couple of very notable exceptions, but I won't be talking about them until much later on). Basically, the chromatic scale looks like this.

A	A#/Bb	B	C	C#/Db	D	D#/Eb	E	F	F#/Gb	G	G#/Ab
1	2	3	4	5	6	7	8	9	10	11	12

What we have here is the 12-note musical alphabet. Despite this description, you'll probably have noticed straight away that there appears to be far more than 12 notes in the diagram. This is one of music's little quirks, where some notes actually have two names. Look between the notes A and B, for instance, and you'll find A♯/B♭ (pronounced 'A sharp' and 'B flat'). In actual fact, this is a single note with two names, and so the note in this position of the chromatic scale can be called one or the other. The reason for this spectacular bout of strangeness is drawn from music's Dark Ages and needn't concern us, just as long that we're aware of it.

The mathematicians amongst you will in all probability be able to work out how many combinations of five-, six-, seven- or eight-note scales it's possible to draw from just these 12 notes without taking off your socks, but the rest of us might need to know that the answer is: lots.

In the past, various nutcases have tried to work out all the variations and combinations and given a lot of them names, which means that the answer to the frequently asked question 'How many scales are there?' is 'More than you could possibly shake a good-sized stick at.' But the good news is that the scales that are in everyday use probably number only four or five. Chief among these is, without doubt, the major scale. This scale is the music foundry that has turned out everything from nursery rhymes to symphonies and a great deal of other stuff in between, so it's fairly logical to assume that the major scale should be our first port of call.

The Major Scale

The first form in which we're going to meet the major scale is in a single-octave version, as shown below. (The term *octave* in this case is just musicspeak for a series of eight notes in a specific order.)

```
C   D   E   F   G   A   B   C
1   2   3   4   5   6   7   8
```

You'll have noticed how the first and eighth notes are both Cs, so most of the time you'll see the above diagram numbered like this:

```
C   D   E   F   G   A   B   C
1   2   3   4   5   6   7   1
```

Whichever way around, it's the same basic information being conveyed.

If you've never encountered scales before, the following diagrams will help you to orientate yourself. Here's the first:

This scale calls for you to start with the second finger on your left hand on the third fret of the fifth string. If you keep your hand in this position, it means that the fingering for the rest of the scale can be kept completely logical and with an absolute minimum of movement in the hand. The second note will be played with your fourth finger on the fifth fret, fifth string. This is followed by the first finger placed on the second fret, fourth string.

Adopting a strict one-fret-per-finger regime is by far the most organised fingering system for playing scales and one that will discipline the hand well, preparing it for playing melody lines and solos later on.

So if we translate the scale above into the other method of notation, we end up with this:

basic Scales For Guitar

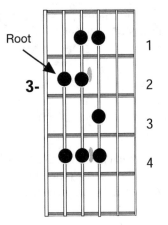

In many ways, the type of diagram shown here is clearer than the tab version because it gives you an essential overview of what's going on, in terms of the shape of the scale on the fretboard. Just like memorising chord shapes on the guitar, it's possible to memorise scale shapes, too. You'll be surprised by how quickly your fingers learn the shapes of scales as well. By practising scales regularly, you're conditioning your fingers to remember a set of reflexive movements that will help you a great deal as a musician. Indeed, playing guitar is a lot to do with reflexes and responses, and this is where the training really begins.

To start with, even a relatively short scale like the one we've been looking at will probably feel awkward to play. You might experience problems co-ordinating your left and right hands, for instance, and for a while you may well find yourself looking at both hands to make sure that your fingers are on the correct strings – and then losing your place on the tab! Don't worry, this happens a lot in the early stages and we've all been there. Before long, this kind of activity is going to feel more and more natural and will eventually become second nature to you, like riding a bicycle. Just take things slowly to begin with. Don't set yourself any unreasonable agendas, and keep reminding yourself that it will take time for your relatively sleepy left hand – which has nearly always played a supporting role to your busier and far more highly trained right hand – to come up to speed.

If you spend two or three minutes playing through this first scale example every time you practise, you'll be doing fine. If you spend too long playing over exercises like this one, you can actually do more harm than good – the scale will become stale and uninteresting, so your mind will wander and all benefit will be lost – so in the early stages just a few minutes a day will be quite good enough. After this, you can go on and play anything you want to and have some fun.

Remember to draw the line between practising and playing. Practising should represent something of a challenge and should always contain something new. Playing is when you merely rake over your repertoire and play everything you know.

What's Next?

The next scale we're going to look at has arguably a lot more to do with rock 'n' roll and blues than the major scale does. It's a five-note scale, and now hang onto your hat – here comes a technical word. This scale is the first in a series of 'pentatonic' scales you'll be looking at. *Pente* is the Greek word for 'five' and *tonic* means 'note', and so *pentatonic scale* merely means 'five-note scale'. Nothing too scary there, I think you'll agree.

Another big difference between the pentatonic scale and the major scale that we've just looked at is that this one is minor. (The difference between major and minor in music is about as vital as gender differences are in life. Whereas the major scale sounds bright and 'happy', the minor scale sounds more subdued and somewhat 'sad'.) Here's the C minor pentatonic scale in tab form:

Now here it is as a fretboard diagram:

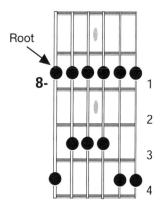

If you play this scale immediately after playing the major scale, you should be able to hear a distinct difference – apart from the fact that this one is shorter than the major, of course!

basic Scales For Guitar

The C minor pentatonic scale contains the following notes:

$$C \quad E\flat \quad F \quad G \quad B\flat$$
$$1 \quad 2 \quad 3 \quad 4 \quad 5$$

As far as the fingering of this scale is concerned, it's a good idea to stick to a similar strategy as before: use one fret per finger. Beware that, in practice, a lot of guitarists use fingers 1 and 3 to play this scale, mainly because of the amount of strength there is in the third finger. This is also the finger that takes care of string bending a lot of the time and, being longer than finger four, it's also got more scope to push the string across the neck. For now, though, it's advisable to keep within the framework that we've already started to establish and make any slight alterations later on. After all, we're not playing music here; it's just scale exercises. This is an important distinction. As I said earlier, a lot of music is drawn from scales, but the scales themselves are about as musical as a telephone book.

When it comes to including this newcomer in your scale-practice routine, all you have to do for now is simply play both scales for a couple of minutes. As your familiarity with each scale increases and your basic co-ordination develops, you should find yourself able to give them a good going over in just a couple of minutes. If not, don't get frustrated; just think of it as a work in progress and tell yourself that people all progress at different speeds.

The Major Pentatonic Scale

Just like ebb and flow, yin and yang, day and night, major and minor scales permeate music and are responsible for a lot of tonal contrast, so it's not surprising that, alongside the minor pentatonic, there's a major pentatonic, too.

The basic breakdown of the C major pentatonic scale would look like this:

$$
\begin{array}{ccccc}
C & D & E & G & A \\
1 & 2 & 3 & 4 & 5
\end{array}
$$

Now here's the tab version of the scale:

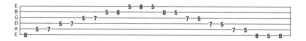

And now here's the fretboard diagram, which I think might cause you to do a double-take:

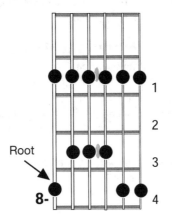

If you're saying to yourself that this diagram looks hauntingly familiar, you're absolutely right. The major and minor pentatonic scales look very similar to each other, but if you check the positions of the two we've looked at on the fretboard you'll notice that they start in very different places. Still, after a couple of weeks of practising the minor version, there's a good chance that your fingers will recognise the shape straight away, which means that you'll be one step ahead in the finger-memory stakes.

Of course, there's a very elaborate and technical reason why these two scale shapes should be so similar to each other, but it's not something I'm going to go into depth about at present. For now, all you need to worry about is making sure that you can play each of the scales we've looked at cleanly.

The Minor Scale

Just as the minor pentatonic scale has a major counterpart in music, the seven-note major scale we looked at earlier has an opposite number in the minor camp, too:

C	D	E♭	F	G	A♭	B♭	C
1	2	3	4	5	6	7	1

Minor scales are not quite as straightforward as majors, in that there are not one but three minor scales available. The one I've shown above is called the *natural minor* scale, and this is the one that is commonly used in most forms of 'popular music', an umbrella term that takes in just about everything except classical music and some of jazz's weirder moments. (I won't be spending too much time on the other two variations on the minor-family theme: the harmonic and melodic versions. For now, just be aware that they exist.) Here's the tab version of the C natural-minor scale:

Now here's its counterpart fretboard diagram:

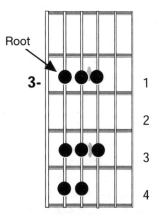

When it comes to adding this newcomer to your scale-practice routine, the most important thing to do is to play the scales consecutively, one after the other, and to try to pick out the differences between them as you do so. By doing this, your ear will begin to develop and vital musical information will start to form inside your head.

I can't stress too greatly how your musical nature has more to do with heart and head than with frets and fingerboard. That is to say that music doesn't start when you pluck a string; it starts with a much earlier process deep inside you. Learning to listen and, more importantly, being able to hear the different tonal variations available to you within these basic scales is a vital foundation on which to build a musical sense, and everything else you learn from this book will be built upon this foundation.

Muscle Beach

Scales do more for you than simply improve your ear; they also do wonders for the developing muscles in your left hand. Add to this that they consolidate the important process of synchronising your left and right hands and you can see that there's a great deal to be gained from spending a few minutes working on them every day.

In order to get the best from your playing, you'll need to tie things together a little more and turn your scale practice into a solid routine. For now, though, let's spend a little time considering the role of the right hand in all of this.

The Right Hand

I'm guessing that you've probably chosen to play guitar using a plectrum. I could be wrong, but this way around is the default for most players – fingerstyle players are comparatively less common – so it's wise to make sure that your choice of plectrum – one of the cheapest pieces of gear you'll ever buy – is right for you.

Plectrums come in an alarming array of shapes and sizes, as a good look at the selection in your local music store will tell you. As far as size is concerned, this is a fairly easy area to get sorted out, as it has little effect on how you play. Plectrum size and physical shape is a very personal thing for guitarists. Most opt for the common triangular shape, but there are other variations that are equally worth considering.

There are large and small plectrums (or plectra, if you're a plural purist), peardrop, teardrop, pointy, smooth – you name it, they're all available – but the only real difference is how comfortable you feel holding them, nothing more. It's not down to how big or small your hands are, either; I've known people with really large hands play with tiny 'mandolin' plectrums, and vice versa.

The best advice here is to experiment. Buy a few differently shaped plectrums and see which one you're most at home with. However, before you actually buy anything, consider the really important variations. These have nothing to do with colour, so feel free to mix and match at will in this department. (I used to tell some of my pupils that white plectrums were louder. I just hope none of them actually believed me.) The actual material from which plectrums are made count a little toward your choice, but once again this is merely a comfort option; plectrums can be made from nylon, plastic, fancy patented variations on plastic and nylon, metal, stone (no kidding – I've got one made from agate) and whatever else can be shaped to fit.

The real determining factor here is thickness. Plectrums vary from a fairly modest .44mm right up to 3mm and beyond. The rigidity of the pick affects your playing in that it aids your control over dynamics (ie loudness and softness). Obviously, hitting a string with a piece of plastic 3mm thick (probably called something like The Exterminator™) is going to set up a whole different set of vibration characteristics in a guitar string than those elicited by a flimsy .44mm pick, so it's thickness that should become the true focus of your plectrum-choosing criteria. Buy a few different picks and find one that suits your playing style.

As a rough guide, most rock players tend to go for heavier plectrums, and anything from .78mm to 1.5mm should do the job just fine. Oh, and remember: the white ones really are louder...

Holding A Plectrum

So, now that you've bought yourself a few shiny new plectrums, you'll be wanting to put them to the test.

First of all, hold the plectrum between your index finger and thumb and let the other fingers on your hand remain relaxed. Don't clench your fingers up into a semi-fist, because this produces tension in the hand, which will actually affect your ability to move it freely. In general, tension is the worst enemy of guitarists, and some will go to almost any length to rid themselves of it – meditation, the Alexander technique, yoga, etc – so don't begin by encouraging any bad habits.

Next, make sure that you're not using too much of the plectrum's tip. About 2mm should suffice; any more and you'll find chords start to sound scratchy and brash. What's more, you'll find yourself having to make small lifting movements with the wrist when playing single notes across strings.

So a plectrum-holding checklist would look something like this:

- Hold between index finger and thumb
- Use only the top 2mm to strike the string
- Keep the hand relaxed
- Keep the wrist as straight as possible

The aim here is to make those movements that are necessary to sound the strings as natural as possible. The body doesn't tend to react too well to being asked to perform tasks that fall well outside its design brief, and so it's in your best interest to give it the easiest possible ride.

Alternate Picking

Now you're ready to play something. Remember that scale shape we looked at a few pages ago? Well, here it is again:

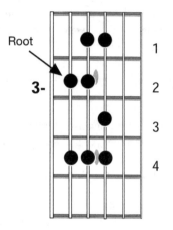

The right way to address playing this scale is by using
a technique called *alternate picking*. This is where the
scale would be started on a downstroke (ie picking
towards the floor) followed by an upstroke for the next
note. This would mean that the scale shape above
would look like this if it were converted into a picking
regime. (It may help you to say, 'Down, up, down,' etc,
as you play through the scale.)

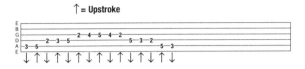

Alternate picking is a very good discipline to adopt right from the word go, despite the fact that you might see guitarists on TV playing with what look like consecutive downstrokes. Just tell yourself that you've got to learn the rules first before you're allowed to break them!

Once you've got your alternate picking working correctly, apply it to all of the scale shapes that we've looked at so far. When everything is running smoothly, you're ready to take things one stage further.

Timing Is Everything

Now we're entering an area that is invaluable for developing excellent technique on the guitar, and I'm afraid it means another trip to the music store.

In order to get the most from your work with scales, you'll need to get hold of either a metronome or drum machine – anything that is capable of keeping a measured beat while you practise. To begin with, set the metronome (or whatever) to around 60 beats per minute and try to play a note of the major scale on every click. You'll only be playing one note per second, so it shouldn't feel too demanding. Be strict with yourself and make sure that your timing is spot on. What you should be hearing is very much along the lines of the following:

note	note	note	note	note	note
click	click	click	click	click	click

Nothing else will do. If you allow any timing indiscretions to go unchecked now, you'll find yourself in a whole world of pain when you try to correct them later on.

When you're sure of yourself at 60 beats per minute, try increasing the speed of the metronome slightly, up to 66 or 70 beats per minute, increasing the speed of the metronome in small amounts. You should never take quantum leaps, because this can trip you up sooner than anything and actually do damage to your developing technique.

Also, be patient. Don't expect to increase the speed of your metronome every time you sit down to practise. These things take time, and a slowly-slowly approach will pay off in the long run.

Speed Trials

Once you've got the idea of playing with a metronome up and running and can manage the likes of 120 beats per minute without too much effort, put the metronome back to 60 beats per minute and try playing two notes per click instead. This means that instead of...

note	note	note	note	note	note
click	click	click	click	click	click

...you'll be playing:

note	note	note	note	note	note
click		click		click	

Remember that it's got to be evenly spaced and in time. If it doesn't sound right, put the metronome back on 120 beats per minute and try playing one note per click again. Mathematically, you're performing the same task both times – one note per click at 120bpm is equal to two notes per click at 60bpm.

Perfecting this means that you now have a further range of metronome speeds to explore, because you can go on increasing the bpm and playing two notes per click right up to 120 again. Once you've achieved this, go back to 60 once again and try to play four notes per click:

note note note note note note note note note note note
click   click   click

Once again, all that's happening here is that you're playing things the way they were when you were playing two notes per click at 120, but now you've taken away another set of rhythmic reference points and you have to be able to maintain perfect timing with less of a guide.

Musically, what you've done is learned the difference between playing quarter notes (one note per click) eighth notes (two notes per click) and 16th notes (four notes per click) – or, if you like, crotchets, quavers and semiquavers. In terms of music notation, it would look like this:

> q = quarter note (one note per click)
> e = eighth note (two notes per click)
> x = 16th note (four notes per click)

This simple set of exercises will act towards giving you a very solid picking technique and an excellent sense of rhythm, two tools that will carry you a long way in guitar music.

Moving On

Naturally, this practice routine will apply to all of the scales found in this book. So far, though, we've looked at only single-octave versions of major and minor scales (the pentatonics were already two octaves long), so the next step with your scale familiarisation is to increase both the major and minor scales to cover a slice of the fretboard, like this:

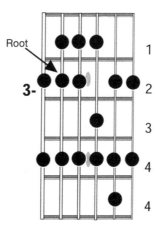

Looks confusing, doesn't it? This is why those in the know use a cross-check between the fretboard diagram and the tab:

The tab should fill in any blanks for you, as it always tells you where to start and finish playing.

When you practice an unfamiliar scale shape for the first time, use the tab to guide you, but try to visualise the actual shape of the scale from the fretboard diagram.

Now here's a two-octave minor scale...

Root

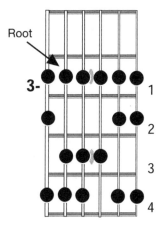

...and here's the tab:

basic Scales For Guitar

It'll probably take you a few days to become familiar with the idea of playing these new shapes, and you might have to wait a while before you try playing through them with the metronome.

When the time comes to put the metronome back into action, start at a very slow speed, perhaps around 80bpm. It's very important to allow yourself time to absorb any new information, and you should never rush to learn more and more as quickly as possible. If inaccuracies are allowed to creep in at this stage, they will be with you for a long time and will eventually take ages to iron out. Be warned!

Once the two-octave versions of the major and minor scales are all up to a reasonable speed, you'll be ready to tackle any of the scales in Section 2 of this book. Be sure to apply all of the same rules as before: try to visualise the shape on the neck, use the tab as a guide to let you know where to start and finish and, to begin with, take things slowly.

My advice is to pick a specific key every time you practise and play all of the scales in that key. For instance, if you chose the key of B, you would practise the major, minor, seventh and both pentatonic scales in that key. The next time, you would do something different. This method is good for your fingers, naturally, but the real benefit will be in providing your ear with the contrasting musical information at hand.

Before you run off, you might like to read the next chapter so that you understand a bit more about where scales come from and how they were formed. There's nothing scary in there, just enough information to temper your musical skills and increase your guitarmanship.

3 WHAT ARE SCALES?

In the previous chapter, we saw how the chromatic scale is music's motherlode, the rich core from which all other scales are drawn. The word *scale* comes from the Latin *scala*, which means 'ladder', while *chromatic* comes from *chroma*, the Greek word for 'colourful', so the scale that contains all of the pitches used in western music is a sort of 'colourful ladder' that climbs from the lowest perceptible notes, at around 20Hz (or Hertz, meaning cycles per second), to the highest. Anything less than 20Hz is felt rather than heard, while the upper limit of your perceptible range could be anything between 16,000Hz and 20,000Hz, depending on how much heavy-metal music you listened to when you were a kid.

I like this idea of using colour, as thinking of music in these terms defines it more as an art form and less of a science, which is how it tends to be treated when taught, in many instances. The many musical series that we draw from the chromatic scale can therefore be seen more readily as being variations in tone, hue or shade, and I believe that this helps students understand better the bewildering array of scales that are available to them. As an example, let's compare two different scales. The first is the major scale, which we've already met:

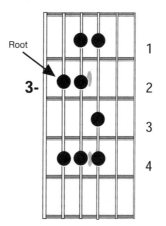

The next scale is known as the 'Hungarian':

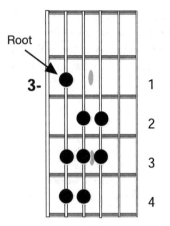

Root

3-

1

2

3

4

They sound vastly different to each other, despite the fact that they're made from similar materials found in the same builder's yard. The defining difference between the two scales is in the actual order and arrangement of the notes that they contain. Let's look at the chromatic scale once again:

A A#/Bb B C C#/Db D D#/Eb E F F#/Gb G G#/Ab
1   2   3 4   5   6   7   8 9   10   11   12

The C major scale we looked at first contains these notes...

C   D   E   F   G   A   B   C

...whereas the Hungarian contains these:

C   D   E♭   F♯   G   A♭   B   C

If we look at this another way and actually define the order of notes in both scales depending on how many frets there are between each of the individual notes, we get this result:

Major Scale

C-D (2 frets)
D-E (2 frets)
E-F (1 fret)
F-G (2 frets)
G-A (2 frets)
A-B (2 frets)
B-C (1 fret)

C major scale along the second string

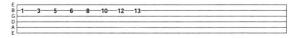

Hungarian Scale

C-D (2 frets)
D-E♭ (1 fret)
E♭-F♯ (3 frets)
F♯-G (1 fret)
A-A♭ (1 fret)
A♭-B (3 frets)
B-C (1 fret)

'Hungarian' scale along the second string

```
E
B--1----3----4----7----8----9---12---13-------
G
D
A
E
```

From this, you can see that scales sound different depending on the distances between each of their individual notes, which are called *intervals*. But, once we've established the note-order templates of each of the different scales – their *keys* – it's easy to work out any scale starting from any given note.

As an example, we've seen what C major looks like, but what if we want a major scale starting on E? If we apply the major-scale template, we get this:

E-F♯ (2 frets)
F♯-G♯ (2 frets)
G♯-A (1 fret)
A-B (2 frets)
B-C♯ (2 frets)
C♯-D♯ (2 frets)
D♯-E (1 fret)

E major scale along the first string

It's hardly surprising, then, that the fretboard diagrams for C major and E major look uncannily familiar:

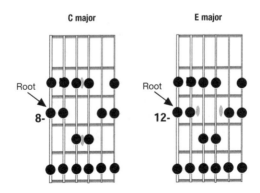

So, as guitarists, we can thank providence that, once we've got the basic fingering pattern (or template) under our fingers, it's really a simple matter of changing location on the fingerboard to explore all 12 major keys rather than learning a completely new fingering each time, which our less fortunate colleagues who have chosen to play piano or saxophone have to do! (Incidentally, if you were wondering exactly where the Hungarian scale comes from, it will probably come as no surprise to find out that it was favoured by some of the Hungarian composers writing during the 19th century, notably Liszt. It's not one we'll be looking at in Section 2, fear not. It's included here simply as an offbeat example.)

The Numbers Game

You might be asking yourself how many scales there are in music, and I must say at this point that I don't know if an exact figure has ever been calculated. I've seen books as fat as telephone directories that list most if not all of them, and I've referred you to the mathematical possibilities concerning the possible permutations of five-, six-, seven- and eight-note scales. But, without a doubt, the question really should read 'How many scales do I need to know?', or even the more honest question 'How few scales can I get by with?'

Bearing in mind that a great many scales are of the highly specialised variety (like the Hungarian, for example) and are not ones that you're particularly likely to find cropping up on a daily basis, I believe that you can cover an awful lot of musical ground with the four scales covered in the previous chapter: major, minor and major and minor pentatonics. Of course, this means that you have to know them in every key, but that's not such a demanding task on the guitar, as we've seen, as the shapes of different scales tend to be very similar. But if you want me to do the maths, here they are:

Major scale x 12 = 12
Minor scale x 12 = 12
Minor pentatonic x 12 = 12
Major pentatonic x 12 = 12
Blues scale x 12 = 12
Dominant scale x 12 = 12

I make that 6 x 12 = 72 – that's one scale for each key multiplied by the number of different scales available to you at this point. When you consider that, once you've learned one fingering template, all you need to do is move it around, the job is cut right down again. The trouble is, you have to learn each of them all over the fretboard.

The Whole Story

Let's look at a few statistics. Your guitar probably has around 20–22 frets, and so knowing this scale...

C major

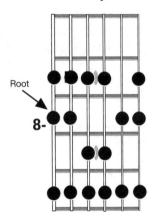

Root

8-

A two-octave scale of C covering four frets – over half of the guitar's range, but only a fifth of the fretboard!

...isn't really telling the whole story. All you've got is four frets' worth of C major, which means that there are another 18 or so unavailable to you in that particular key. In order to solve this problem, we divide the fingerboard up into five lumps, like this:

The five-piece guitar-fretboard jigsaw.
Notice how the tops and bottoms of the
various scale shapes 'interlock'

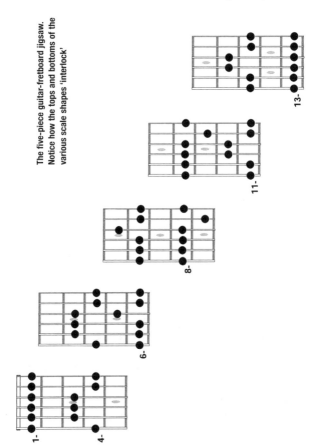

These five shapes are actually enough to cover the entire fretboard, because after the 12th fret everything starts repeating again:

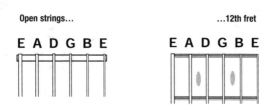

Open strings...   ...12th fret

E A D G B E   E A D G B E

And so every scale is split up into five locations on the fretboard which fit together like jigsaw pieces and ensure that each key or scale type is adequately represented at every point along the way.

Unlocking The Keys

Some keys in music are more common than others. In jazz, for instance, the 'flat' keys – B♭, E♭, A♭ and so on – tend to predominate, but this has got very little to do with the music itself. It's actually down to the fact that horn players (trumpet, sax and trombone players, etc) find the flat keys easier to play in – B♭ especially – and, seeing as jazz started off being defined by horn sections and, later on, by solo sax players, B♭ tends to be the default jazz key. It's not a fantastically easy key for pianists and guitarists, of course, but at the time, that didn't matter; the horns dominated the jazz landscape and only the strong survived.

But when it comes to guitar music, we tend to find songs written in keys with easy chord shapes – C, D, G, E and so on – and so it's advisable to look at scales in these keys first. Because of the fact that the scale shapes all repeat in the various keys on the guitar fretboard, you'll find that, once you're familiar with a few of the more guitar-orientated keys, the rest aren't too difficult to come to terms with. Good luck!

SECTION 2

4 MAJOR SCALES

C Major Pentatonic

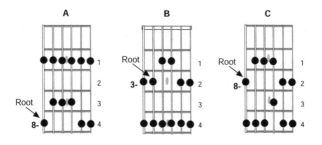

A

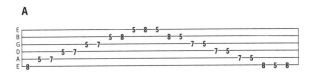

B

C

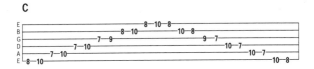

D

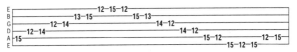

E

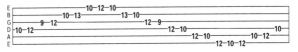

C#/Db Major Pentatonic

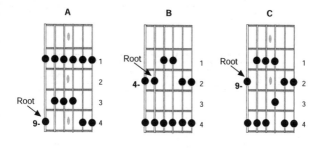

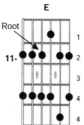

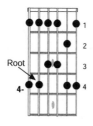

A

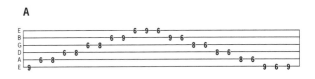

B

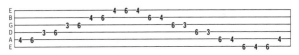

C

D

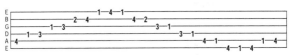

E

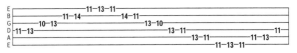

D Major Pentatonic

A

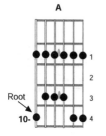

B

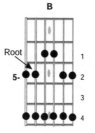

C

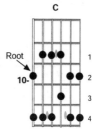

D

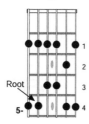

E

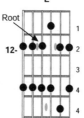

A

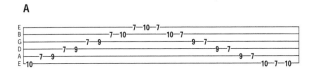

B

C

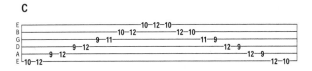

D

E

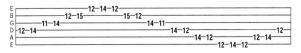

D#/Eb Major Pentatonic

A

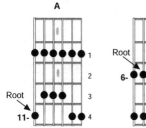

B

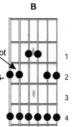

C

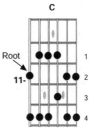

D

E

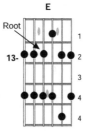

A

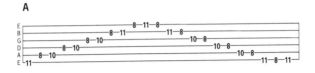

B

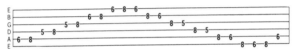

C

D

E

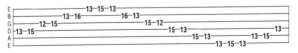

E Major Pentatonic

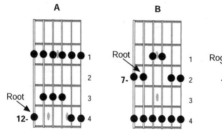

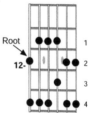

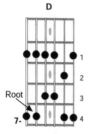

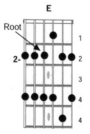

A

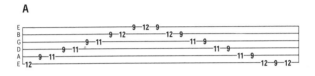

B

C

D

E

F Major Pentatonic

A

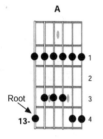

B

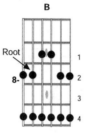

C

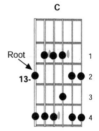

D

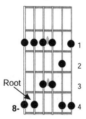

E

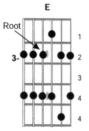

A

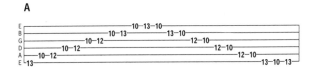

B

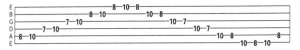

C

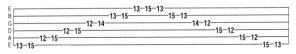

D

E

F#/Gb Major Pentatonic

A

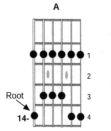

B

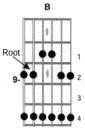

C

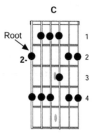

D

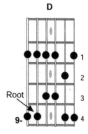

E

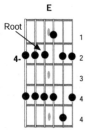

A

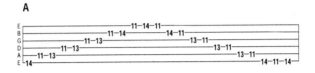

B

C

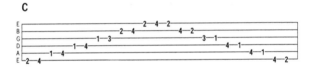

D

E

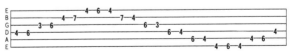

G Major Pentatonic

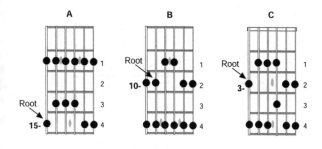

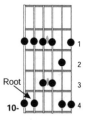

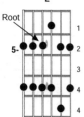

A

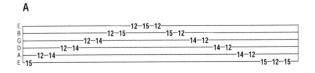

B

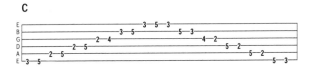

C

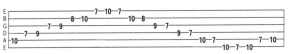

D

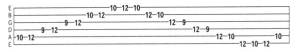

E

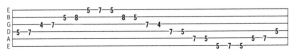

G#/A♭ Major Pentatonic

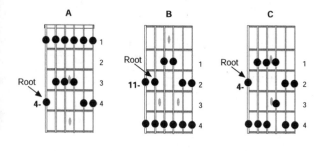

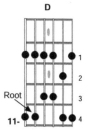

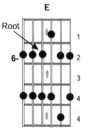

A

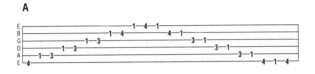

B

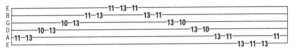

C

D

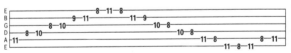

E

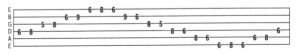

A Major Pentatonic

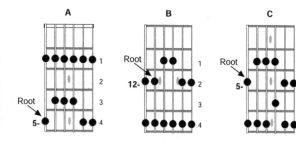

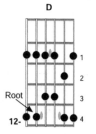

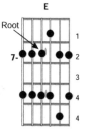

A

B

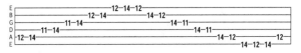

C

D

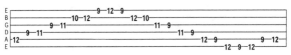

E

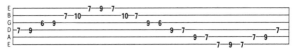

A#/Bb Major Pentatonic

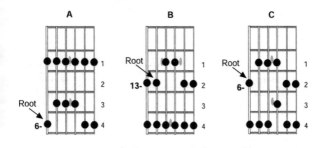

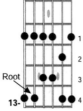

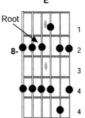

A

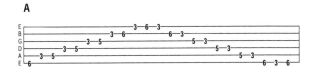

B

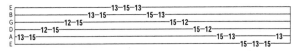

C

D

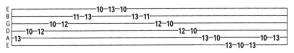

E

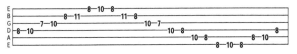

B Major Pentatonic

A

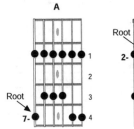

B

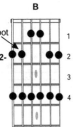

C

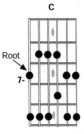

D

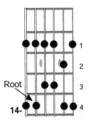

E

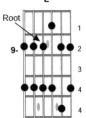

A

B

C

D

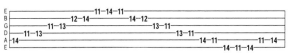

E

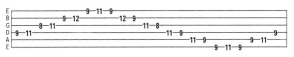

C Major

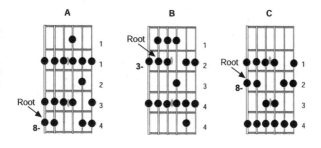

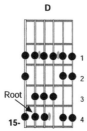

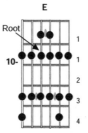

A

B

C

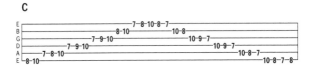

D

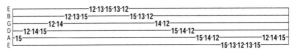

E

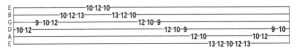

C#/Db Major

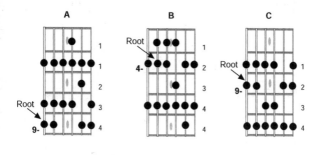

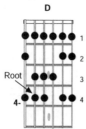

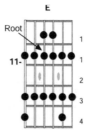

A

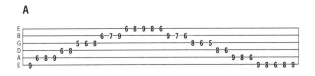

B

C

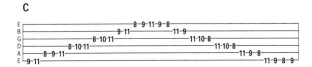

D

E

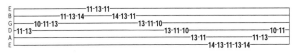

D Major

A

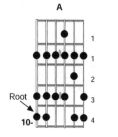

B

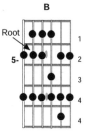

C

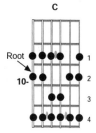

D

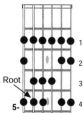

E

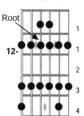

A

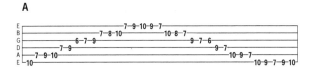

B

C

D

E

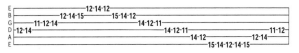

D♯/E♭ Major

A

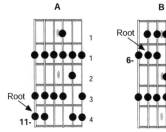

B

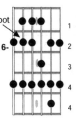

C

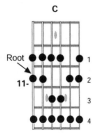

D

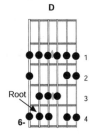

E

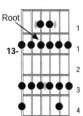

A

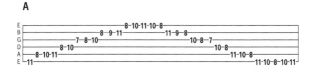

B

C

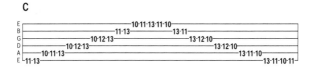

D

E

E Major

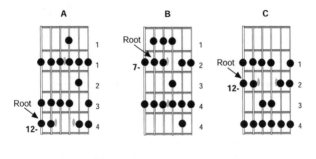

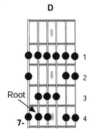

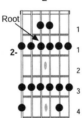

A

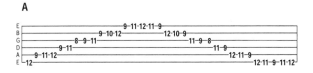

B

C

D

E

F Major

A

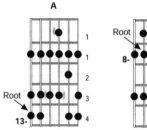

B

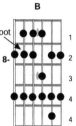

C

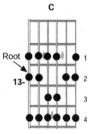

D

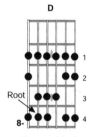

E

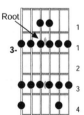

A

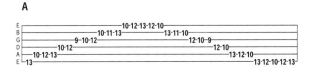

B

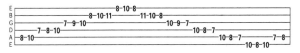

C

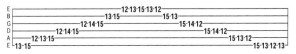

D

E

F#/G♭ Major

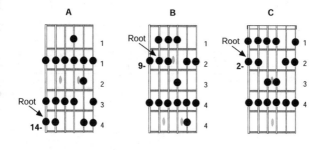

A

B

C

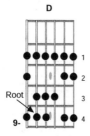

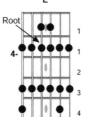

D

E

A

B

C

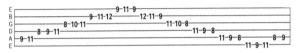

D

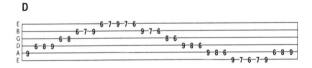

E

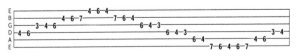

G Major

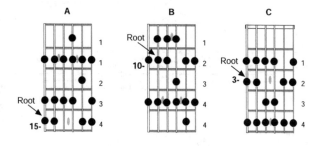

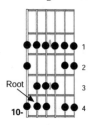

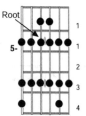

A

B

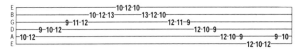

C

D

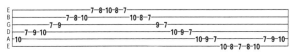

E

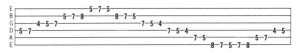

G#/Ab Major

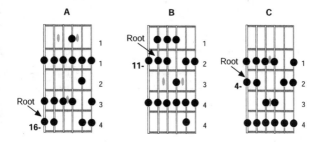

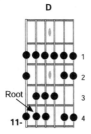

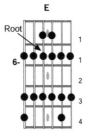

A

```
                                        13-15-16-15-13
E ─────────────────────────────────────────────────────────────────
B ─────────────────────────13-14-16──────────16-14-13──────────────
G ──────────────12-13-15──────────────────────────────15-13-12─────
D ──────────13-15───────────────────────────────────────────15-13──
A ────13-15-16─────────────────────────────────────────16-15-13────
E ──16────────────────────────────────────────────16-15-13-15-16───
```

B

```
                                    11-13-11
E ─────────────────────────────────────────────────────────────────
B ───────────────────11-13-14──────────14-13-11────────────────────
G ──────────10-12-13──────────────────────────────13-12-10─────────
D ──────10-11-13─────────────────────────────────────────13-11-10──
A ──11-13──────────────────────────────────────────13-11-10───10-11
E ──────────────────────────────────────────────13-11-13───────────
```

C

```
                        3-4-6-4-3
E ─────────────────────────────────────────────────────────────────
B ──────────────────4-6──────────6-4───────────────────────────────
G ──────────3-5-6──────────────────────6-5-3───────────────────────
D ──────3-5-6──────────────────────────────6-5-3───────────────────
A ──3-4-6───────────────────────────────────────6-4-3──────────────
E ──4-6─────────────────────────────────────────────6-4-3-4────────
```

D

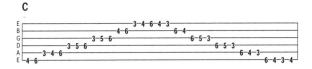

```
                        8-9-11-9-8
E ─────────────────────────────────────────────────────────────────
B ──────────────8-9-11──────────11-9-8─────────────────────────────
G ──────────8-10──────────────────────10-8────────────────────────
D ──────8-10-11──────────────────────────11-10-8───────────────────
A ──11─────────────────────────────────────────11-10-8────8-10-11──
E ──────────────────────────────────────────11-9-8-9-11────────────
```

E

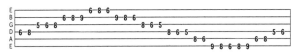

```
                        6-8-6
E ─────────────────────────────────────────────────────────────────
B ──────────────6-8-9──────────9-8-6───────────────────────────────
G ──────5-6-8──────────────────────8-6-5───────────────────────────
D ──6-8──────────────────────────────────8-6-5─────────────5-6─────
A ─────────────────────────────────────────────8-6──────6-8────────
E ──────────────────────────────────────────9-8-6-8-9──────────────
```

A Major

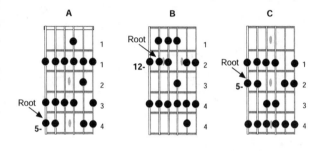

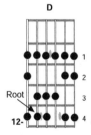

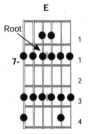

A

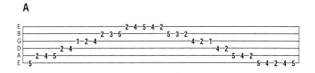

B

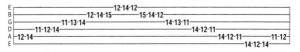

C

D

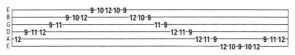

E

A#/B♭ Major

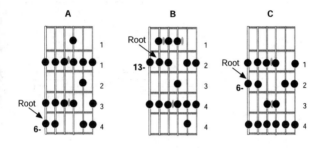

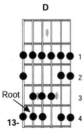

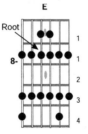

A

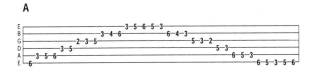

B

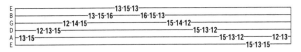

C

D

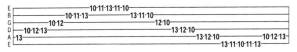

E

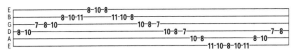

B Major

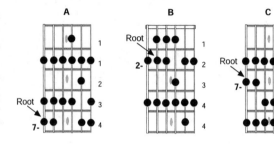

A

B

C

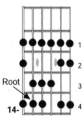

D

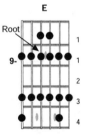

E

A

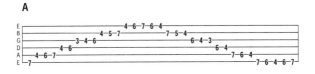

B

C

D

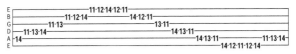

E

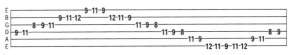

5 MINOR SCALES

C Minor Pentatonic

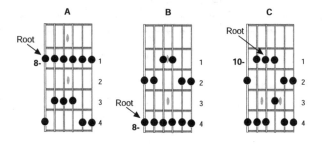

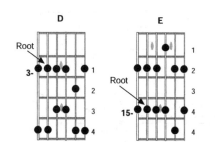

A

B

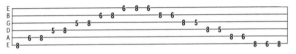

C

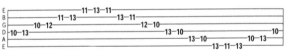

D

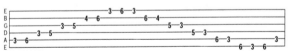

E

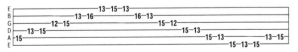

C#/Db Minor Pentatonic

A

B

C

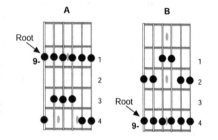
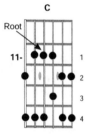

D

E

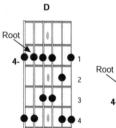
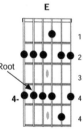

A

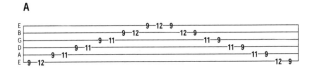

B

C

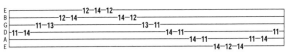

D

E

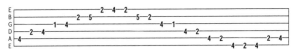

D Minor Pentatonic

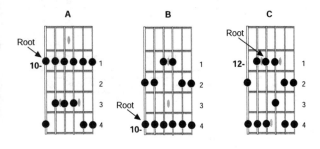

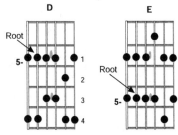

A

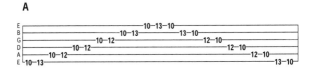

B

C

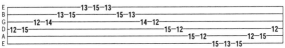

D

E

D#/Eb Minor Pentatonic

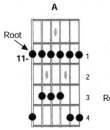

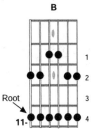

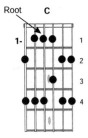

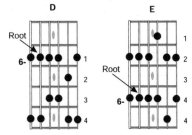

A

B

C

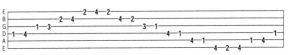

D

E

E Minor Pentatonic

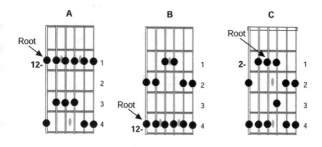

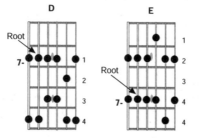

A

B

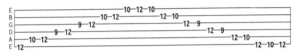

C

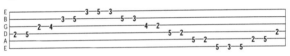

D

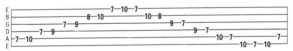

E

F Minor Pentatonic

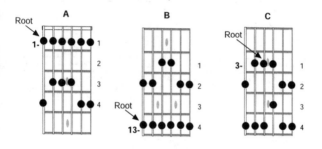

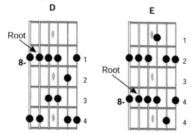

A

B

C

D

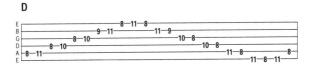

E

F#/Gb Minor Pentatonic

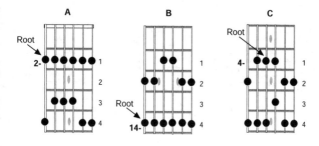

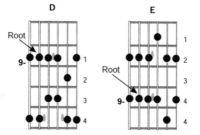

A

B

C

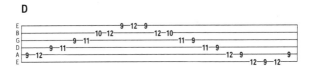

D

E

G Minor Pentatonic

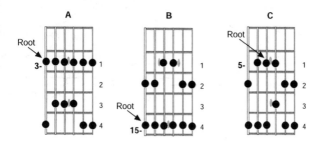

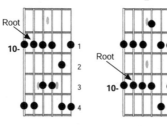

A

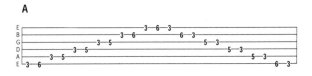

B

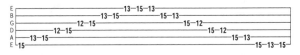

C

D

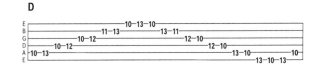

E

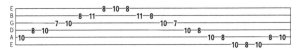

G#/A♭ Minor Pentatonic

A

B

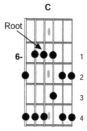

C

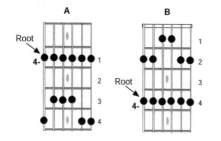

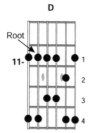

D

E

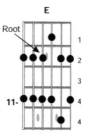

A

B

C

D

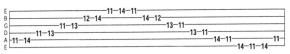

E

A Minor Pentatonic

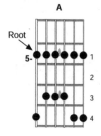

A

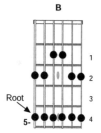

B

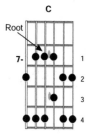

C

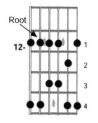

D

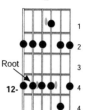

E

A

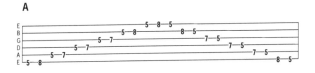

B

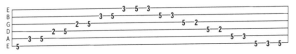

C

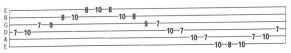

D

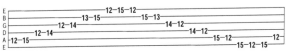

E

A#/Bb Minor Pentatonic

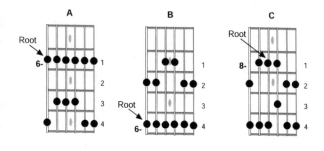

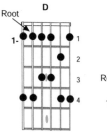

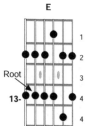

A

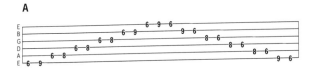

B

C

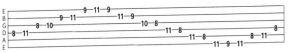

D

E

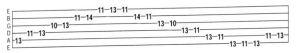

B Minor Pentatonic

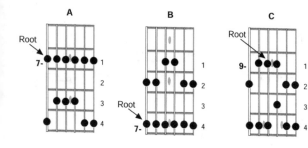

A

B

C

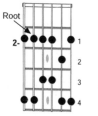
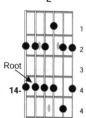

D

E

A

B

C

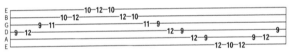

D

E

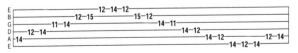

C Natural Minor

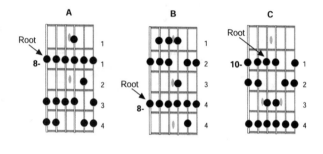

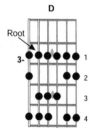

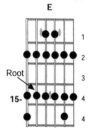

A

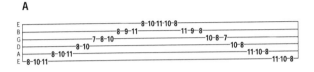

B

C

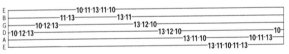

D

E

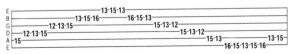

C#/Db Natural Minor

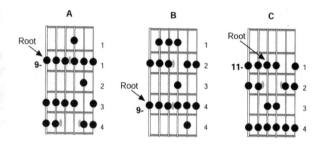

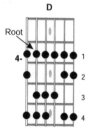
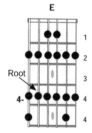

A

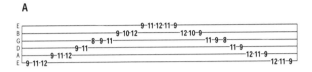

B

C

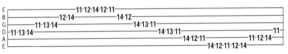

D

E

D Natural Minor

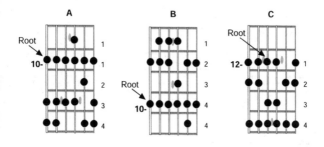

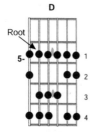

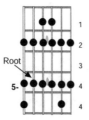

A

B

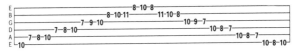

C

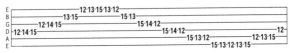

D

E

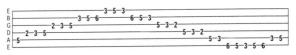

D#/E♭ Natural Minor

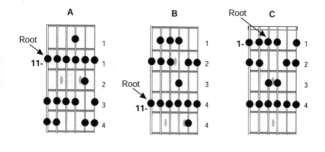

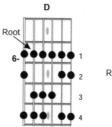

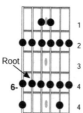

A

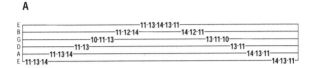

B

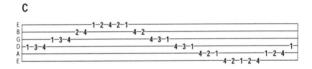

C

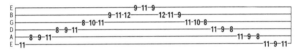

D

E

E Natural Minor

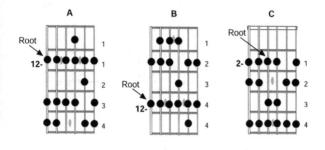

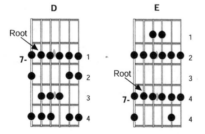

A

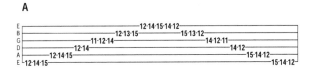

B

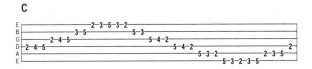

C

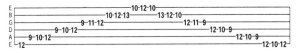

D

E

F Natural Minor

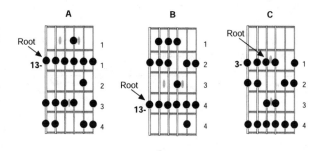

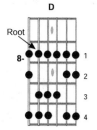

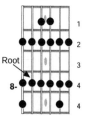

A

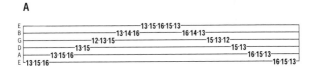

B

C

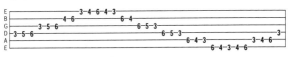

D

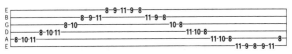

E

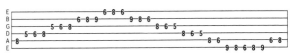

F#/G♭ Natural Minor

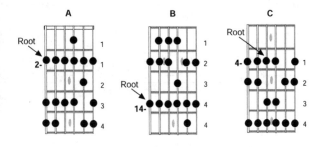

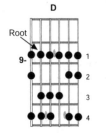

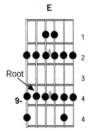

A

B

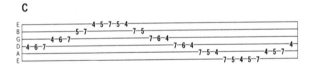

C

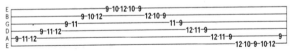

D

E

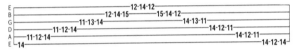

G Natural Minor

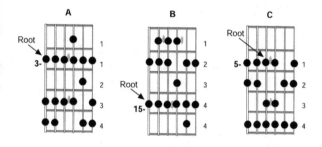

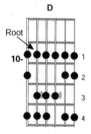

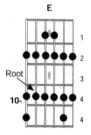

A

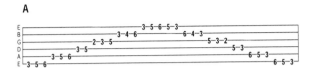

B

C

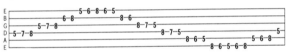

D

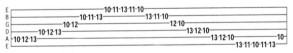

E

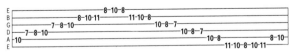

G#/A♭ Natural Minor

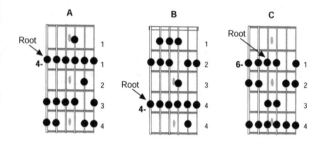

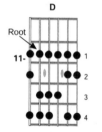

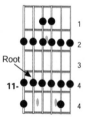

A

B

C

D

E

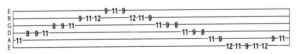

A Natural Minor

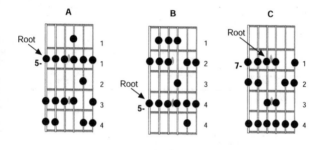

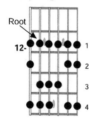

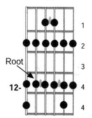

A

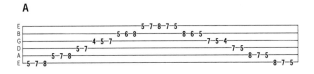

B

C

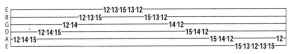

D

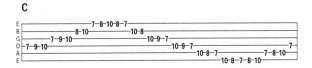

E

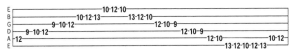

A#/B♭ Natural Minor

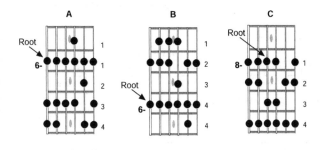

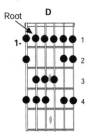

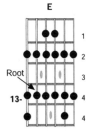

A

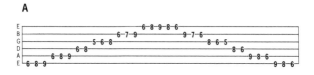

B

C

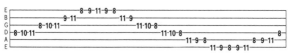

D

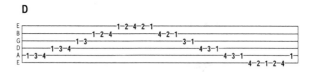

E

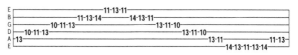

B Natural Minor

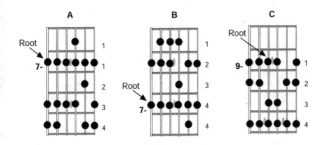

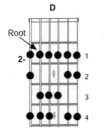

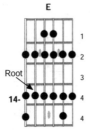

A

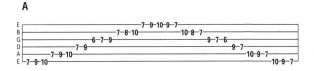

B

C

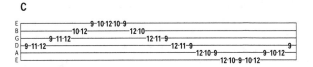

D

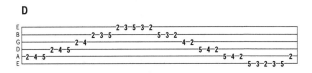

E

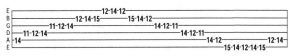

6 DOMINANT SCALES

C7

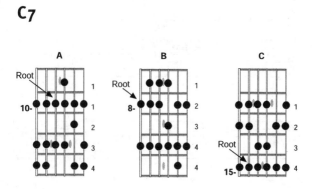

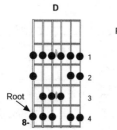

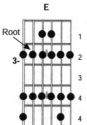

Dominant Scales

A

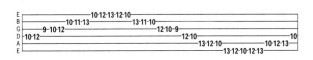

B

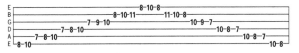

C

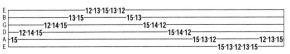

D

E

C♯7/D♭7

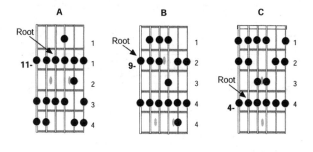

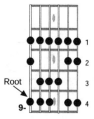

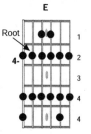

A

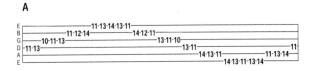

B

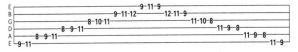

C

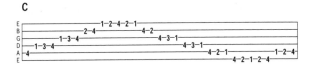

D

E

D7

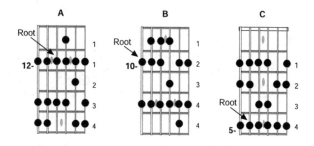

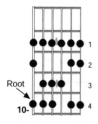

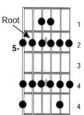

A

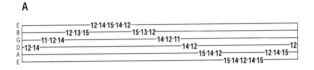

```
E|--------------------12-14-15-14-12--------------------------------------------|
B|--------------12-13-15------------15-13-12----------------------------------|
G|---------11-12-14-----------------------14-12-11---------------------------|
D|-12-14-------------------------------------------14-12-------------------12-|
A|----------------------------------------------------15-14-12-----12-14-15----|
E|----------------------------------------------15-14-12-14-15-----------------|
```

B

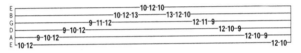

```
E|------------------------10-12-10-------------------------------------------|
B|------------------10-12-13--------13-12-10-------------------------------|
G|-------------9-11-12----------------------12-11-9------------------------|
D|--------9-10-12--------------------------------12-10-9-----------------|
A|----9-10-12--------------------------------------------12-10-9---------|
E|-10-12------------------------------------------------------12-10------|
```

C

```
E|--------------------2-3-5-3-2--------------------------------------------|
B|-----------------3-5-----------5-3------------------------------------|
G|-----------2-4-5------------------5-4-2------------------------------|
D|------2-4-5-----------------------------5-4-2----------------------|
A|---5-----------------------------------------5-3-2-------2-3-5------|
E|--------------------------------------------5-3-2-3-5--------------|
```

D

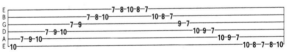

```
E|--------------------7-8-10-8-7------------------------------------------|
B|-----------------7-8-10----------10-8-7----------------------------|
G|-----------7-9--------------------------9-7------------------------|
D|------7-9-10---------------------------------10-9-7--------------|
A|---7-9-10--------------------------------------------10-9-7------|
E|-10----------------------------------------------10-8-7-8-10----|
```

E

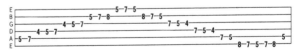

```
E|--------------------5-7-5------------------------------------------------|
B|-----------------5-7-8----------8-7-5----------------------------------|
G|-----------4-5-7--------------------7-5-4----------------------------|
D|------4-5-7----------------------------------7-5-4------------------|
A|---5-7-----------------------------------------------7-5-------5----|
E|------------------------------------------------8-7-5-7-8----------|
```

D#7/E♭7

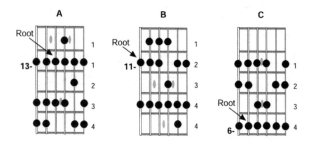

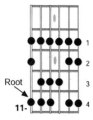

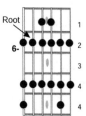

A

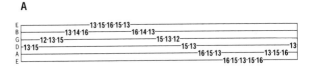

B

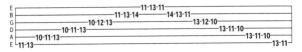

C

D

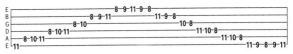

E

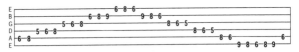

E7

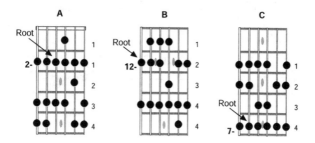

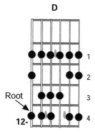

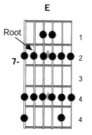

A

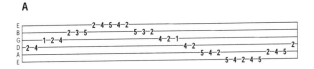

B

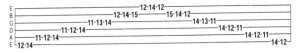

C

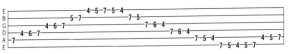

D

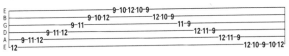

E

F7

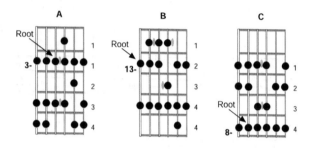

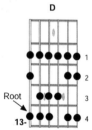

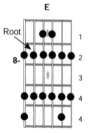

A

B

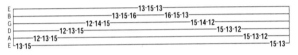

C

D

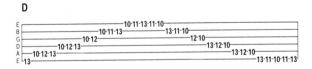

E

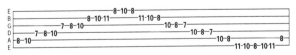

F#7/Gb7

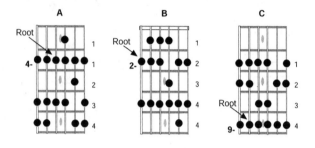

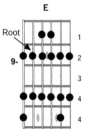

A

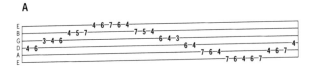

B

C

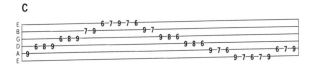

D

E

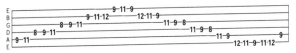

G7

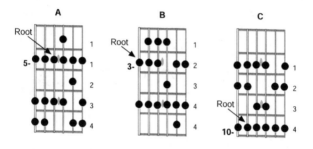

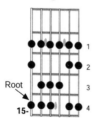
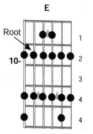

A

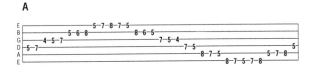

B

C

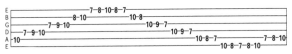

D

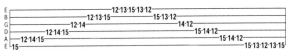

E

G#7/Ab7

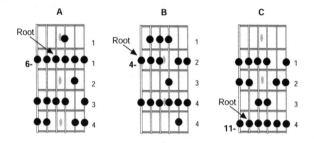

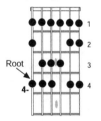

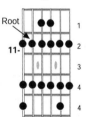

A

```
E |-------------------6-8-9-8-6-----------------------------------|
B |-----------6-7-9----------------9-7-6-------------------------|
G |------5-6-8-------------------------------8-6-5--------------|
D |--6-8------------------------------8---------------------6--|
A |-------------------------------------9-8-6----------6-8-9----|
E |------------------------------9-8-6-8-9----------------------|
```

B

```
E |-------------------------4-6-4-------------------------------|
B |-----------------4-6-7--------------7-6-4--------------------|
G |------------3-5-6----------------------6-5-3----------------|
D |--------3-4-6---------------------------------6-4-3---------|
A |----3-4-6-------------------------------------------6-4-3---|
E |--4-6----------------------------------------------------6-4|
```

C

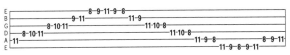

```
E |-------------------8-9-11-9-8--------------------------------|
B |-------------9-11----------------11-9-----------------------|
G |------8-10-11-----------------------------11-10-8----------|
D |--8-10-11---------------------------11-10-8----------------|
A |--11--------------------------------------11-9-8----8-9-11--|
E |-----------------------------------11-9-8-9-11-------------|
```

D

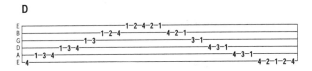

```
E |-------------------1-2-4-2-1---------------------------------|
B |-------------1-2-4--------------4-2-1------------------------|
G |----------1-3----------------------3-1---------------------|
D |------1-3-4----------------------------4-3-1---------------|
A |--1-3-4--------------------------------------4-3-1---------|
E |--4----------------------------------4-2-1-2-4------------|
```

E

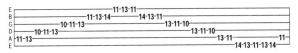

```
E |-------------------11-13-11----------------------------------|
B |-------------11-13-14---------14-13-11----------------------|
G |------10-11-13-------------------------13-11-10------------|
D |--10-11-13----------------------------13-11-10------------|
A |--11-13-------------------------------13-11----------11---|
E |-----------------------------------14-13-11-11-13-14------|
```

A7

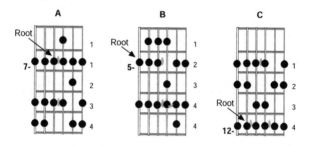

A

Root

7-

1
1
2
3
4

B

Root

5-

1
2
3
4
4

C

12-

1
2

Root

4

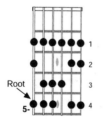

D

Root

5-

1
2
3
4

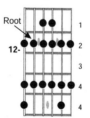

E

Root

12-

1
2
3
4
4

A

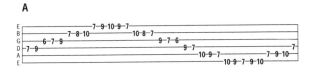

B

C

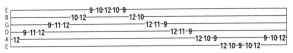

D

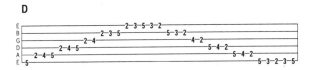

E

A♯7/B♭7

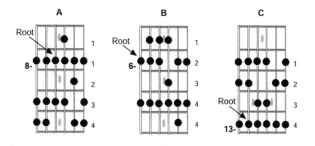

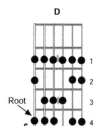

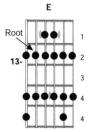

Dominant Scales

A

B

C

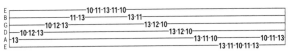

D

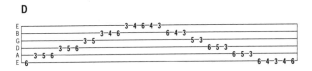

E

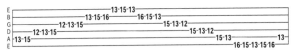

B7

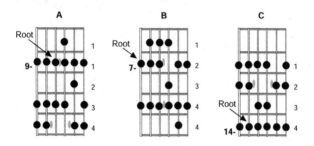

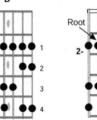

A

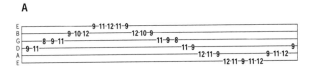

B

C

D

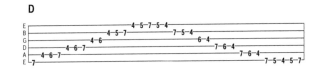

E

APPENDIX 1
The Blues Scale

I think it's a shame, in many ways, that there has to be anything like a 'blues scale', in the academic meaning of the word. The *blues* is far more free-form than that. It didn't spring from a textbook – no music originated that way – and so applying some kind of formula to it, or pinning it down with a set of predictable principles, seems wrong.

In actual fact, I believe that the blues actively resists any attempt to regulate it into a teachable medium and playfully confounds traditional music theory at many points along its course as part of its skittish nature.

In any case, scales are always a bit 'after the fact' in that they're the result of a form of analysis that sets out to reduce a particular music form to its most basic common denominator and, as such, end up not really representing the music at all. A comparison would be reducing a work of classic fiction – Dickens, Mann, Shakespeare – to a set of component parts. You'd come to the conclusion that they all used a selection of nouns, verbs, adverbs, pronouns and so on – and, if you really wanted to reduce it still further, that they all used the alphabet. Now, I'm anticipating that everyone out there knows the alphabet back to front – we all had to recite it from kindergarten onwards – but how many of us could write a book based solely on that knowledge?

Scales are studied mainly to provide students of music with a sort of handrail to guide them through certain melodic criteria that apply to music in general and their instruments in particular. The theory is that, if you're familiar with all of the colours in the paintbox, you'll be able to paint prettier pictures.

When it comes to the blues, however, all theoretical staples have to be put on hold. It's not a music form that conforms to any of music's laws; indeed, most of the chords in use in the blues tend to be dominant sevenths, a predominance of which is something not found in any other music style and definitely contrary to the basic ideas regarding harmony. What's more, the blues scale as such uses notes that aren't otherwise found in western music.

To explain all this, it's necessary to delve into music's

innards for a couple of paragraphs. The squeamish among you are invited to find something to hold onto. Remember when we met the chromatic scale, earlier in this book? Here it is again, just to save you a lot of unnecessary page flipping.

A	A#/Bb	B	C	C#/Db	D	D#/Eb	E	F	F#/Gb	G	G#/Ab
1	2	3	4	5	6	7	8	9	10	11	12

Here you see 12 notes, all mathematically the same distance from each other, in terms of pitch. In other words, the gap between, say, C and C# is exactly the same as it is between G and G#. This means that, if you looked at how many cycles per second (Hertz) your guitar string vibrated when you plucked a C and then again when you plucked a C#, the exact same ratio would be present if you compared G and G#.

So the chromatic scale is really mathematically uniform throughout its range, and the smallest gap between two notes – the distance between C and C#, etc – is called a semitone. But this wasn't always so. Before the maths majors and PhD (Mus) guys got hold of it, the chromatic scale was a little more erratic in that it wasn't exactly uniform. Far from it, in fact. Believe it or not, around 600 years ago, the key of D major would have sounded different to C major not only in terms of pitch but also in the way in which the notes within both scales related to each other.

During the 16th century, lutenists (our guitar ancestors) would have had frets made from gut tied at the back of the instrument's neck and repositioned according to key – much more of a hit-and-miss affair than our perfectly regulated chromatic system of today. In fact, the first part of many lute suites from that era were written in such a way that the performer could test the tuning of his instrument – a sort of early-music soundcheck!

So How Does All Of This Relate To The Blues?

When the chromatic scale was finally sorted out and organised so that all of the notes therein were equal to each other, anything less than a semitone was abandoned – but only in the west. In eastern, oriental and African music, the gaps between notes were often far smaller than the western standard semitone. These gaps are referred to as *microtones* by the academics, and in the normal course of things you shouldn't come across them – unless, of course, you want to study sitar or any of the instrumental traditions east of Europe. However, there are microtones present in the blues and they are of vital importance to us as musicians because of the effect that they have on blues music.

The reason why microtones crop up in blues is because the blues is based on some African musical traditions that were imported into the southern states of the USA during the shady days of the slave trade. In those days, African natives were effectively kidnapped from the country's west coast by unscrupulous slave traders and put to work in the plantations of the USA's Deep South. They weren't allowed any possessions and any evidence of their indigenous culture was strictly taboo.

The slave population's musical heritage couldn't be denied, though – it ran too deep – and so, when it came to singing in the fields, although their own tribal songs were disallowed, any attempt at singing western songs revealed fully the cultural differences between the two nations.

Musicologists have found that the microtonal qualities of the blues existed in the musical traditions of western Africa, and it's the influence of this chromatic schism that gives the blues its principal propellant.

To understand what's happening more fully, here's the C minor pentatonic:

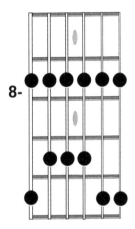

The notes affected by the microtonal anomaly are the third and fifth, shown in the diagram over the page:

basic Scales For Guitar

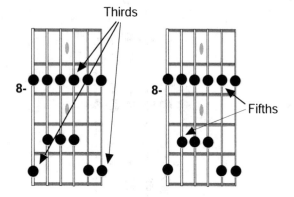

The fact is that neither of these two notes are a true pitch, according to the western system. The third, for instance, is not this...

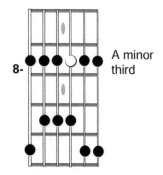

A minor third

...or this:

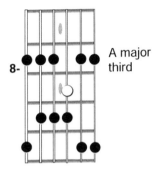

A major
third

Instead, it's somewhere in between, which is something that we guitarists can take full advantage of because we can bend the string here...

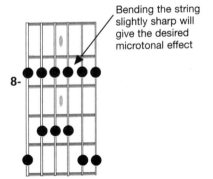

Bending the string
slightly sharp will
give the desired
microtonal effect

...until it sounds bluesy enough. It doesn't get as far as the next semitone along...

Bend towards the pitch at the ninth fret,
but let the note fall slightly short of the target

```
E
B
G ----8----(9)----
D
A
E
```

...but instead falls very slightly short.

The same is true for the fifth. It's not always 'spot on', in terms of pitch; it's more often than not at an indeterminate point between here...

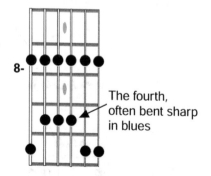

The fourth, often bent sharp in blues

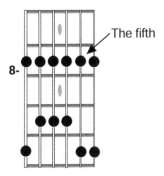

...and here:

So, in order to make the blues scale sound 'right', these anomalies in pitch must be observed, and if you're sufficiently conversant with the blues by ear then you should be able to make enough of an adjustment.

Are Five Notes Enough?

So, is the blues scale really just five notes? In my opinion, no.

One way of determining the scalebase of a form of music is to write down every note from a melody in that particular style and see what you've got as a series of common denominators. In this way, I've determined that the pentatonic scale with added indeterminate pitches just isn't enough; there's more.

Take a look at the formula for the minor pentatonic scale:

C   E♭   F   G   B♭

In musical terms, we're using the root, minor third, fourth, fifth and flat seventh. But there are blues melodies out there that contain sixths and ninths, too, and there are plenty of players, from Robben Ford to BB King, who make full use of them. So, shouldn't the blues scale look a bit more like this?

C	D	E	F	G	A	B♭	C
1	2	3	4	5	6	♭7	1

And if we allow for the microtonal pitches...

C	D	E♭/E	F	G♭/G	A	B♭	C
1	2	♭3/3	4	♭5/5	6	♭7	1

This scale is far more representative of the music in general, if you make the correct allowances for the indeterminate pitches. In fact, it bears a certain resemblance to the dominant-seventh scale, which we looked at earlier in the book. You've just got to be aware of where the microtones fall.

Meanwhile, the minor pentatonic scale is useful as a means to getting you into the blues ballpark and will definitely serve you well as an initial means of providing a perfectly respectable solo during your early endeavours. As your ear develops, however, you'll find yourself wanting to include more elements from the other scales in this book into your bluesy melodic outings.

APPENDIX 2
Faraway Scales With Strange-Sounding Names

Of course, this isn't the end of the story, by any means. The scales covered in this book are those that are in common use and are vitally important for you to include in your musical vocabulary, but there are others.

As I said earlier in the book, if you want to take a mathematical stance on how many scales there are in music, you've only got to see how many ways you can split the chromatic scale into series of five-, six-, seven- or eight-note groups and give each of them a name. Most of them will sound very strange indeed, but it might fill a rainy afternoon when you're tired of teasing the cat.

Any further study of scales falls outside the scope of this book, but I thought that it might be fun to introduce you to a few more (at least in theory) to give you a good idea of what lies ahead, should you wish to pursue your studies in music. For instance, if

Faraway Scales With Strange-Sounding Names

I told you that there is a Scottish pentatonic scale,
you might not believe me, but nevertheless it exists.
Here it is, in fact:

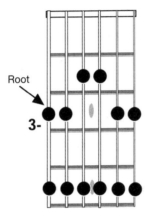

If you play the above example, you might be able to
hear a certain Scottish lilt to it. In fact, a lot of Scottish
folk music is derived from this scale. And you might
not be too surprised to hear that the bagpipes are
tuned to a pentatonic scale, too.

basic Scales For Guitar

Another pentatonic variation that turns heads sounds distinctly Indian:

Root

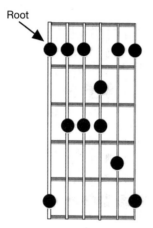

I don't know if the scale above is called the 'Indian pentatonic' or not (probably not), but it sounds uncannily familiar – especially if you've been listening to George Harrison's 'Within You, Without You' from the excellent *Sgt Pepper's Lonely Hearts Club Band* album!

These are just two examples of scales that you don't really need to know but are fun to play with, all the same. Mind you, I guess you'd need to know the Scottish pentatonic if you were going to study traditional Scottish folk music, and the Indian pentatonic would probably prove to be a real showstopper at your next evening out with friends at the curry house.

Modes

You might have heard talk of 'modes' or 'modal scales' before and wondered what they were. A dictionary definition reveals that modes are 'states of being', and I think that that's pretty much right, especially if you apply it to the major scale.

Looking once again at the C major scale in its basic state, we have this order of notes:

```
C   D   E   F   G   A   B   C
1   2   3   4   5   6   7   1
```

This represents the normal 'state of being' for the major scale. But what happens if we start to play the scale from D?

```
D   E   F   G   A   B   C   D
```

basic Scales For Guitar

Basically, we've discovered a new scale. Well, we haven't, because this scale has been around for hundreds of years – long enough, in fact, to have a Greek name: the Dorian. It's exactly the same as the C major scale and nothing like the D major or minor scales, so in that respect it's something different.

Taking this idea one step further, try playing the C scale from another note and see what happens.

E F G A B C D E

This mode of the major scale is known as the Phrygian (pronounced 'Fridge-Ian') and has a Spanish feel to it. Try sounding an E minor chord and playing it over the top and you'll see what I mean.

You've probably guessed that there are more modes available from the major scale, and so here's quick run-down.

Modes In C Major

C	D	E	F	G	A	B	C	*Ionian*
D	E	F	G	A	B	C	D	*Dorian*
E	F	G	A	B	C	D	E	*Phrygian*
F	G	A	B	C	D	E	F	*Lydian*
G	A	B	C	D	E	F	G	*Mixolydian*

Faraway Scales With Strange-Sounding Names

```
A  B  C  D  E  F  G  A      Aeolian
B  C  D  E  F  G  A  B      Locrian
```

Of course, the modal idea and naming system isn't exclusive to the key of C major; it applies to all major scales. I could have just as easily shown you the list like this:

```
1  2  3  4  5  6  7  1      Ionian
2  3  4  5  6  7  1  2      Dorian
3  4  5  6  7  1  2  3      Phrygian
4  5  6  7  1  2  3  4      Lydian
5  6  7  1  2  3  4  5      Mixolydian
6  7  1  2  3  4  5  6      Aeolian
7  1  2  3  4  5  6  7      Locrian
```

So, any major scale played from its third note to the note of the same name an octave higher would be known as the Phrygian mode of that particular root.

You've already come across three of these modes during the course of reading this book: the Ionian is mode another name for the straight major scale, the Mixolydian is the same as the dominant scale and the Aeolian is the same as the natural minor. That leaves you with four more to explore, should you wish to do so. However, as I say, this sort of thing falls outside this book's agenda of providing you with a basic grounding in the most important scales.

Minors Aloud

You can apply the same logic to the minor scales, too. The minor that we've looked at – the natural minor – is one of the major scale modes, but if you apply the same idea to the melodic minor scale you end up with another seven modes, and the same goes for the harmonic minor, too. The resulting modes aren't taught in conventional music, but they seem to have attracted names and operating practices, mainly from jazz academics, although I won't overload you with their names here. Just be aware that this is how the modal system works – it's merely another way of looking at something you've already met.

Looney Tunes

From here on in, you'll get to meet some of music's more eclectic variations. Earlier, I looked briefly at the Hungarian scale, and a lot of the scales left in the box are built along very similar lines. They're representative of a certain musical culture that's been reverse-engineered down to a selection of notes that best represent them.

There are man-made scales (as opposed to what, I wonder?) like the diminished and augmented, in which the intervals have all been arranged symmetrically. In the case of the augmented, there's a tone between each note, while in the diminished the gaps alternate between a semitone and a tone, as shown below.

Both of these scales sound particularly nasty, from a melodic point of view, and in my opinion represent music analysis gone haywire.

Augmented

Diminished

Root

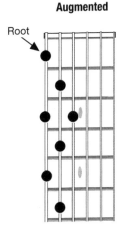

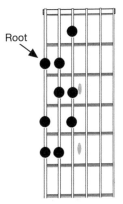

The whole-tone scale, one of music's more symmetrical moments

The diminished scale – let's face it, not at all pretty

Turning Japanese

There are also Japanese pentatonic scales, although these merely skim the surface of a very complex musical structure that cannot be fully explained in western musical terms. The Kumoi, Hirajoshi and Iwato scales will give you a glimpse of oriental musical thinking but are very far from the full story.

A Little Light Reading

Those of you who have become fascinated with the variety of musical scales on offer may wish to peruse one or two books on the subject. Possibly the most famous was written by a Russian-born musicologist called Nicolas Slonimsky, who wrote a book called *The Thesaurus Of Scales And Melodic Patterns*, which will introduce you to some of music's more fantastic areas. However, be warned! It's heavy going and tends to do things like turn you on to jazz...

Meanwhile, I hope that this book has helped you in your initial foray into the inner workings of music. With the scales included here under your belt, you're well prepared for most of the melodic information that will come your way in popular music. Hopefully, too, your fingers will be more familiar with the fretboard, your ears more tuned in to music in general and the foundations of your musical personality dug deep.